WINGS OF A FREE BARD

A Medley of Poetry for Happiness and Harmony

By
VARCHASWI L. PUTCHA

ALL RIGHTS RESERVED

All rights reserved. No part of this publication may be reproduced, stored in or introduced into a retrieval system, or transmitted, in any form by any means may it be electronically, mechanical, optical, chemical, manual, photocopying, or recording without prior written permission of the Author.

WINGS OF A FREE BARD

Poetry by
Varchaswi L. Putcha
Ph: +91 99483 56626
E-mail: varchaswi.official@gmail.com

Copy Right:
Varchaswi L. Putcha

Published By: Kasturi Vijayam
Published on: Feb-2024

ISBN (Paperback): 978-81-966116-2-0

Print On Demand

Ph:0091-9515054998
Email: Kasturivijayam@gmail.com

Book Available
@
Amazon, flipkart

DEDICATION

I dedicate this anthology to my beloved mother, ***Smt. Putcha Prabhavathi***, who has inculcated in me the habit of book reading and encouraged me to write, and who has been a constant source of support in all my successes.

-Varchaswi L. Putcha

ACKNOWLEDGEMENTS

My profuse thanks to **Dr LSR Prasad**, a poet laureate with an authorship of more than 200 books in Telugu and English languages, for readily agreeing and providing a beautiful Foreword.

My thanks to **Dr.Jayadev**, a retired professor, animator, most renowned cartoonist and poet, with whom I have a long association and friendship, who too has readily provided a few lines of blessings on this anthology.

Also, my thankful blessings to my better half *Vijaya Nandini* for her support from the domestic front and to my son **Srisai Hriday Tej**, daughter **Srihamsini Duddu**, and son-in-law **Satyanarayana Duddu** for their constant encouragement.

My sincere thanks go to **Sudhir Reddy** of Kasturi Vijayam and his team who associated in publishing the book.

-Varchaswi L. Putcha

BRIEF BIO OF VARCHASWI L. PUTCHA

Varchaswi L. Putcha is a poet, artist, and writer from Hyderabad, Telangana, India. He has a remarkable talent for sketching, cartooning, and caricaturing, and has won many awards at the national and international level. He retired in August 2023 as a Senior Superintendent in the Good and Services Tax Department of the Central Government, Hyderabad and is currently a practicing advocate of the High Court of Telangana State.

He is a prolific writer of short stories in Telugu, and published an anthology of short stories, Varchasweeyam, in 1997. He is also a bilingual poet in Telugu and English, and published an anthology of Telugu poems, Lokaassamastha, in 2014. His compilation of cartoons, Varchaswi Cartoonlu, was published by EMESCO in 2017. He is an illustrator, painter, and poet all rolled into one and has carved a niche for himself.

He is a free thinker and an ardent humanist with a pragmatic approach. His works, whether in prose, poetry, painting, or cartooning, not only carry amazing aesthetics and hilarious satire, as also angst for the deprived and downtrodden and glorification of humanism and humanity. On the educational front, he holds a Bachelor of Science and a Master's degree in both Sociology and Law.

FOREWORD

VARCHASWI SOARING ON HIS WINGS OF POETRY

'-A pen never bends before anything on earth
But renders its thoughts on the white sheets-'

Varcha nama mahatejah Soma putrah pratapavan
Sobhimanyu nrusimhasya phalgunasya suto bhavat
— *Mahabharatam- 12-5-18*

A Leo by birth and well known as Varchaswi by pen and brush deeds, Putcha Lakshminarayana Varchaswi is a popular poet, artist, illustrator, cartoonist, caricaturist, bard and storyteller from Hyderabad. Born in the middle of Baby Boomers Generation with ruling planet sun and birthstone ruby, he is like the flower larkspur of delphinium dabbling with colours pinks and yellows with sagebrush toxicity against social ills.

As could be seen from this book **'WINGS OF A FREE BARD'-A medley of Poetry for Happiness and Harmony'**, his verses and lines are universally ceremonious. At times stately. The movements at times easily anticipated. His style is simple yet passionate and marked by economy and concentration. Sharp intense image is this poet's best instrument. He combines considerable learning with an enlightened understanding of the people and he expresses the lives of people in a witty way of concealed seriousness.

The Lord of his planet- Apollo the god of oracles, healing, music and arts, archery, light, knowledge bestowed on him certain gifts prolifically and allowed him to lead the way and to fulfil the secret desire to be a star among the peer. His contribution to Telugu fine arts were - in 1997- Varchasweeyam- a collection of short stories, in 2014- Lokassamasthaa- a collection of poems and in 2017- Varchaswi cartoonlu- a pocket book collection of social cartoons.

He is a guy of multiple faces and appropriate masks. He nibbles the lines with contemporary parables and dribbles the caricatures with phantastic facsimiles in a nimble way. He is a pen in-law and bar-at-law. His exercises were with the Central Excise Department that explains his incisiveness and wit in collecting and conceding GST(Goods and Services Tax) in smiles and similes seamlessly in day-to-day good service under metaphoric acts.

In this anthology he has penned 40 poems in English that encompass various genres and situations. With pen and ink that were at his command to churn out lines that every nib would be jealous of, he flies high like a twin winged bird of poetry and cartooning-

Yes, It's a bird and bard only
who can fly smoothly
traversing the humongous literary seas
and meandering the galaxies of poesies
                              - Fly Smooth…

A poem begins as an impulse and acquires a heart of its own pulsating in emotional holy see. The controlled development of the poet's talent the finality and the grace of statement is- like a line a connection of two expressive points, and so a poem is a connection of two things. See his anguish and pain roaring in a verbal storm...

That's the damn outrage on the womanhood
Vulturous attack on our holy culture
A mayhem on the motherhood
drawing shameless contours of nation as a sepulchre ...
...O' Shameless Toms, Dicks and Donkeys
Where are you taking my land
by grabbing the modesty of enriched values!
Where are you taking my Nation
by parading naked your atrocities!
Where are you taking my pious motherland
by injuring the dignified souls holding half the skies!
                                            -The Naked Parade

The grimness and awfulness and untouchable sadness of things both in the world and in the self, rue for justice and roar for peace. He pines and wishes ...

Let neighbourhoods bloom like a poem in spring and pen a sonnet of unity and amity to sing. Why do you and I pluck our hairs? When we could love and grow; Why do we hurt and fight each other? When we could heal and glow!

There is pictorial vividness and narrative skill in his poetry. His ability to bring his erudition within the range of general understanding, his versatile and sensitive craftsmanship and his use of rhythm as a fluid instrument of verse demonstrated a range of possibilities. In his Villanelle- **Upright** - he chisels a lovely villa with his pen –

> *Even a broomstick retains its worth*
> *Bends only to sweep the dust under the sheets*
> *A pen never bends before anything on earth*
>
> *Only when they lose their strength or girth*
> *They bow to time to suffer under its cleats*
> *A pen never bends before anything on earth*
> *A creeper bends only when loses its berth*
>
> **- Upright**

The muse mulls over the success of Space Odyssey of Bharat, oversees the 'overseas love', feels like a tiny Savory delight crunched behind the folds of her beautiful lips and concludes that he subsumed himself into the eternal love and global peace across. In his poem – Painting - he describes vividly the sacred ritual of painting in polytonal style...

> *Drawing one's painting or portrait is a sacrament pious!*
> *It's an ensconcing the throne of Lord, the Creator;*
> *It's a re-molding by the Creator;*
> *A true exposition to a brush's enigma; Consecrating blooms of colored quills;*
> *A silent bedaubing of adulations on canvas;*
> *A manifestation of an ineffable supreme meditation! –*

The art of art, the glory of expression and the sunshine of the light of the letters is simplicity. (Walt Whitman). The fruition of beauty is no chance of hit or miss. Like Rodolphe Toffler the father of comic strips our poet Varchaswi writes symphonically associating themes and melodies with great freedom and suggestiveness on the large and unending qualities of the man himself.

Three limericks twinkle like stars in this anthology sky...
one sparkles like this...

A cine star who had liposuction
To act in a film of princely portion
A poet mended a bit his way
Got a good readership hooray
Lo, both made their best version

-Best Action

Poems like **shawl, walk of life, stay safe** are commentaries on contemporary vigour and rigours of life. **Hilarious gales, brush, poor sparrow, in the fist of times, Yoga and Isolation** dwell in philosophical lanes like **the migrant birds at Nelapattu**.

The poet says-

a cartoonist in me ventures to draw a doodle!
With no symphony or harmony in lives,
a malady instead a melody, plays always malice
Yet he alone faces the music, in distress
as these waves of the music go tremulous
and bouts of tremors   knock out him
while the wavelengths score incoherent chime!

-Wavelengths at seas or concerts

He has created his poetry as a gifted nonprofessional, passion for perfection in ideas of order with sensuousness and primitive wonder.

Tolls in 'noose' paper, Online classes, purse versus Priapus, Beats, Cell phone are some poems that mirror the present-day society.

Varchaswi tried his hand at translating other well-known poets' poems successfully. **Of Doves-** Shri Uppaluri Atreya Sarma, **Slithered Mirror-** by Poet Asha Raju- **Each article a Penny!** - by Dr S V Satyanarayana; **A foot-path appears-** by Dr. K. Siva Reddy; **A little while-** by Afsar Mohammed; **The rain-bow that loved me-** by Late Sri Devipriya; **Amaranth-**by late Dr. Dasarathi-

I am sure this poet's anthology will reach vast audience through his artistic talent, keen political perception, devastating satire, inventive genius, and unquenchable conviction.

As the essence of the book, in hand
Gives effervescence of inexplicable thrill and knowledge
and as the tome widens the dome of wisdom, in grand
Those gushes of epitome quench me as a salvage!
                                              -Booklet

Apoorvo bhati bharatyah, kavyamruta phale rasah
Charvane sarva samanye, swaduvit kevalam kavih
                                        -Bhojarajeeyam.

Dr. Lanka Siva Rama Prasad
Warangal.
Cardiothoracic surgeon, Writer, Poet, Artist, Cartoonist, Animator, Philanthropist.

INTRODUCTION

Varchaswi's superhit cartoon book "VARCHASWEE CARTOONLU" was an enthralling experience as I had penned the foreword. When he asked me to share my thoughts on his anthology, which is a reader's delight, currently on my reading table, I felt happy and all the more mesmerized.

We love poetry, cartoon art and have been friends for decades. Our forebrains get charged up with flashes of creativity and we sail smoothly on rivers of imagination and mutual admiration. Varchaswi is a bilingual poet. His wealth of vocabulary in Telugu and English is enormous and his phraseology is chiseled with pun and fun in equal measures. He nurtures a rare talent in writing a sonnet or a free verse. English or Telugu, the alphabets dance to the tunes of his pen.

He translates one to the other with equal ease, the theme remaining intact. It is a rare feat that not many are capable of. In this beautiful book of poems, Varchaswi proves his mettle with choicest words, the rhymes and rhythms, forming a caduceus in absolute tranquility. Here is an example:

Here is an example:

"To be a superman is what a Man pined for
Sci-tech proved him reach beyond the greater blues
Landed in Southern side moon that hitherto has no clues
So, I surpassed a poor bird since long
Passed all tests of racketeering in a bang

Wings, wings and wings
That surrendered to human fancies
that remained a strong desire still;
for a poor bard to get into its mantle!
Then his pen plumed into feathers
Began flying in all poetic weathers
Wings, wings, and wings"

fly smooth

Further, all his poems are enriched by his lovely doodling or drawing that stands special and unique to this anthology. I am sure his poetry connects consistently with the readers and elevates their aesthetics. I wish the author success, and may he publish more of his work to the lovers of poetry.

Prof Dr.Jayadev,
Writer, Poet, Cartoonist, Caricaturist, Animator.

PREFACE

'Poetry is the spontaneous overflow of powerful feelings. It takes its origin from emotion recollected in tranquility' - as quoted by William Wordsworth. Precisely, it is the feeling or emotion recollected in tranquility and accordingly this exercise is a sort of showcasing my feelings in tranquility resulting in a posse of poems like this, as a maiden collection of my reflections.

For me, being an 'Artoonist'(*a blend/ portmanteau, of Artist and Cartoonist*), writing poetry is a manifestation of angst against the lopsided elements that played the social fabric of a welfare state. This could have been drawn out or purged of my conscience pretty well by my drawings, artworks, or short stories, *per se.* Then why hang on to poetry?

Let me present a quote by Horace here: "A picture is a poem without words." This gives us a picture of a picture pulling a poem into its fold. Fine. Then what about a poem? We have an excellent amalgamation of both painting and writing in this famous quote by Plutarch: "Painting is silent poetry, and poetry is painting that speaks".

After giving adequate thought to this, it seems to me that 'cartooning' has a canvas mostly to roll out matters of scorn or fun or both, as accepted widely across the readership, and 'art or painting' has a canvas predominantly for aesthetics whereas the kind of a canvas for poetry is a serious, crisp, sonorous, metaphoric and damn decent one to the extent of classiness and ultimately poetry should acquire the quality of - painting that 'speaks'!

Having said this, taking up the task of penning the poetry appeared to me to be a daunting one with my limited and mediocre knowledge of the prosodic and metric rules meant for the English poems of different genres. I am delighted to say that my humble endeavors in the past few years in laying a rookie hand on this puzzle, thanks to the association I sparingly had with my Telugu and English poets, came out as a pleasant surprise in the form of a booklet in your hand, with an expectation to get a good amount of motivation from a wider section of readers in further pursuance of my poetics.

Dr LSR Prasad, the globally famous poet laureate, has given a bewildering appraisal of this little and humble work with all the required analyses of my lines in his mesmerizing and prodigious way of presentation. I am sure that I am lucky to have his blessing words that spur the readers to browse the book in a kind and passionate state of mind, which I feel would result into an added applause to me.

In this preface, it appears that I do not have much to put forth, after the maestro in his 'foreword' has dwelt-in with the niceties and nuances at length, since he already introduced my work in terms of its tinge, approach, genre, craft and mindset put in, *et cetera*. I can only say that the sublime of my work you see, if any, is nothing but a result of magnanimous and rich quality of reading you have; and any kind commissions and omissions found are definitely my drawbacks to be addressed to, at my end.

This apart, I would like to submit that the set of my drawings or illustrations for each of the poems flown from my 'brush' is expected to give a value addition to my 'pen' in paving the way for a happy and harmonious reading. I solicit the readers to inbox their kind, valuable, considered and critical comments to my mail-id provided in the first page.

Varchaswi L Putcha

WINGS OF A FREE BARD

1. FLY SMOOTH — 2
2. THE NAKED PARADE — 4
3. ALL PALS — 8
4. HIDE AND SEEK — 10
5. UPRIGHT — 14
6. SPACE ODYSSEY OF BHARAT — 18
7. THE MUSE OVERSEAS — 20
8. I FEEL LIKE…… — 24
9. ETERNAL LOVE — 28
10. PAINTING — 30
11. WALK OF LIFE — 32
12. SHAWL — 34
13. STAY SAFE — 36
14. HILARIOUS GALES — 38
15. BRUSH — 40
16. POOR SPARROW — 44
17. IN THE FIST OF TIMES…! — 46
18. MIGRANT BIRD AT NELAPATTU — 50
19. TRAIN THE THOUGHTS — 54
20. GAIETY OF MY CITY — 56
21. WAVELENGTHS AT SECONCERTS — 60
22. YOGA AND ISOLATION — 64
23. TOLLS IN 'NOOSE' PAPER — 66
24. ONLINE CLASSES — 70
25. PURSE Vs PRIAPUS — 72
26. BEATS — 74
27. BOOKLET — 76
28. I AM — 78

29.	BEST ACTION	82
30.	'ONE MORE ROUND' OF A LIMERICK	84
31.	A DROP	86
32.	APPLICATION	88
33.	'CELL' PHONE	90
34.	OF DOVES	94
35.	SLITHERED MIRROR	96
36.	EACH ARTICLE A PENNY!	98
37.	A FOOT-PATH APPEARS	102
38.	A LITTLE WHILE	106
39.	THE RAIN-BOW THAT LOVED ME	108
40.	AMARANTH	112

Varchaswi L. Putcha

WINGS OF A FREE BARD

A Medley of Poetry for Happiness and Harmony

FLY SMOOTH

Wings, wings, wings...
which give things swings, swings and swings
Tempted by a bird to fly far and far;
To be a superman is what a Man pined for
Sci-tech proved him reach beyond the greater blues
Landed in Southern side moon that hitherto has no clues
So I surpassed a poor bird since long
Passed all tests of racketeering in a bang
Wings, wings and wings
That surrendered to human fancies
remained a strong desire, still;
For a poor bard to get into its mantle!
Then his pen plumed into feathers
Began flying in all poetic weathers
Wings, wings, and wings
Yes, It's a bird and bard only
who can fly smoothly
traversing the humongous literary seas
and meandering the galaxies of poesies

Varchaswi L. Putcha

THE NAKED PARADE

With A for arson and B for butchering
that's taught and learnt on social slates-
Where else would morals end up stooping
and how can ladies be respected as deities!

She could be anyone on the burning altar
Day before it's Bilkis Bano,
followed by the cruel murder of poor Sakshi
Yesterday Disha too was ravaged so!

And today a few brutal hands crushed
some petals of lilies of Manipur;
Values and ethics of land got bruised
when civilization goes into a stupor

Dastardly bastards or bloody brats;
Wild boars or predators with heinous acts
Anti-social or ugly outfits
Name them as you deem fit

Varchaswi L. Putcha

Wings Of A Free Bard

That's the damn outrage on the   womanhood
Vulturous attack on our holy culture
A mayhem on the motherhood
drawing shameless contours of the nation as a sepulcher

clefts in casts, rifts in religions
strife in sects, drifts in morals
fissures in friendships
tussles in selfish rulers

All these, badly let loose
abuse on the modesty of womanhood
and none knows when these crimes reduce
For sure, such molestations need a nip in the bud

O' Shameless Toms, Dicks and Donkeys
Where are you taking my land
by grabbing the modesty of enriched values!
Where are you taking my Nation
by parading naked your atrocities!
Where are you taking my pious motherland
by injuring the dignified souls holding half the skies!

Varchaswi L. Putcha

ALL PALS

Mulling to pen a pretty poem on a pal
is like filling hearts with thrills of intimacy.
No exception to the sweet ties of Indo-Nepal
while inking a well synced cultural legacy.

When sagas of our friendship are so long,
a reminiscence of it brings joy forever.
From Shakya to Prachanda harking back all along
is a nice heritage that brings folks nearer.

Troubled ripples may crop up in a serene pond
by a pelt of guileful stone from a shore, bellicose.
Yet, warmful treatises keep us in a strong bond
and a healthy tete-a-tete brings peace we chose.

Let the neighborhoods bloom like a poem in spring
and pen a sonnet of unity and amity to sing.
   (A sonnet)

Varchaswi L. Putcha

HIDE AND SEEK

The golden sun plays hide and seek
With the twinkling star in the night

A green plant cuddles a red tulip
With a fragrant kiss in the light

A towering mountain and a swampy fen
Entwine their peaks and roots

A babbling brook and a twisting stream
Mingle their waters and shoots

A gentle shower and a fierce storm
Romance with rain and thunder

Azures and rubies smooch in the sky
With colors of wonder

Rosy dawn and chilly dusk
 Hug with warmth and grace

Smooth silk and crackling fire
Dance with swirls and lace

Varchaswi L. Putcha

Why do you and I pluck our hairs?
When we could love and grow

Why do we hurt and fight each other?
When we could heal and glow

Varchaswi L. Putcha

UPRIGHT

A pen never bends before anything on earth
But renders its thoughts on the white sheets
A creeper bends only when loses its berth

Even a broomstick retains its worth
Bends only to sweep the dust under the sheets
A pen never bends before anything on earth

A flower of fragrance too, in mirth
Never stoops to fall on the streets
A creeper bends when loses its berth

A bird in flight looks behemoth
and never falls from cloudy sheets
A pen never bends before anything on earth

A star has light, and no dearth
And never lost in the darkest skies
A creeper bends only when loses its berth

Wings Of A Free Bard

Only when they lose their strength or girth
They bow to time to suffer under its cleats
A pen never bends before anything on earth
A creeper bends only when loses its berth

(A villanelle)

Varchaswi L. Putcha

SPACE ODYSSEY OF BHARAT

When Bharat shoots up like a star so bright
in the galaxy of nations far and wide
traversing in perfect orbits day and night
gave Chandrayan-3 a hitting success with pride

The comity of nations gave applause so loud
harking our rocketry, in a grand stupor
Our scientists' fitting toil from this soil made us so proud
made Bharat's space probe a super-duper

With each launch, we reach new heights so high
and inspire generations to come so true
Our space explorations made nations bonsai
What, in the future, we discover in space has no clue

Yes, we progress to reach a Shiv-Sakthi point
While on Mars and beyond, and leave our foot-print

(A Shakespearian sonnet)

Varchaswi L. Putcha

THE MUSE OVERSEAS

I sit at this shore,
You are far off, on the other side of seas.

So what?
When I tweak your shyness here,
I could see your blushed cheeks there.

When I send my rays of desire across the waves,
I see you seduced there, by their embrace.

When I throw my chuckles here,
I see you weave them in your hair.

The corals I courier by waves to you,
Adorn your neck-line like jewel, new.

Each ivy of my poems that I craft here
Causes your skin to tickle and laugh there

Varchaswi L. Putcha

One thing is sure, my dear,
My tidal wave that rises high for you this shore,
Will reach and splatter you there, for sure.
And we will reunite in bliss, I swear.

Varchaswi L. Putcha

I FEEL LIKE……

I feel like a tilting Lilly
In the brooks of your smiles.

I like to be a sparkling chrysanthemum
In your lascivious cheeks.

I like to be the music of your ivory throat
That adorns your gorgeous face and azure braid.

I feel like the blaze of heat
That erupts from your lovestruck breath.

I feel like drops of nectar
That spring from your lips of fire.

I feel like a sari roll skirting the breast line
Of your portrait of the great Cupid.

I feel like a golden girdle encircling
The waist of your poetic beauty.

I feel like a tiny savory delight crunched
Behind the folds of your beautiful lips.

ETERNAL LOVE

I surrendered all my words to birds
Lost all my feathers of dialects except chirps of bards

Plunged my lusts into the vast seas
Now I am a formless onelike tossed fizzes pious

I put off the haste swords into the staid scabbards
Now picked paint-brush and pen for hordes

I bulldozed the castles of cast crass
Now I effulge like aleader of the vibrant mass

I subsumed myself into eternal love and global peace across
Now I don't have time and place except love

Varchaswi L. Putcha

PAINTING

Drawing one's painting or portrait is a sacrament pious!
It's an ensconcing the throne of Lord, the Creator;
It's a re-moulding by the Creator;
A true exposition to a brush's enigma; Consecrating blooms of coloured quills;
A silent bedaubing of adulations on canvas;
A manifestation of an ineffable supreme meditation!
An offering a cherished harmony in high honor;
Placing a diadem of pied rainbow on the pate;
Besmearing an unguent of chef-d'oeuvre;
Chiseling out strangely the demeanors of dearest!
Transmitting nascent sunbeams of gleaming artistry;
Cuddling once again the palpitating palettes;
Doodling those darlings in cozy curves;
Featuring the object into matured expression;
Providing a palatable portrait in pomp; Pumping oxygen to the newfound portrait;
Stroking a graceful plumage with a brush stroke;
Congratulating, by dousing those hearts won, in hues and colors!

WALK OF LIFE

I walk
behind her rhythm, my eyes plant 'there' like a tattoo!

I happened to be always 'behind' for years
nay, for ages
without a contact, eye to eye

Times rolled Tides too tired
The walk continues dying from behind her!

One day, I dumbstruck on listening to somebody from
my behind bombarding at me
'Why won't you look back ever even while she was
groping your shadow in warmth
from behind for ages?' and
'Why should she tattoo your mien on the time-line
of her swaying waist-line?'

Yes, a walk-of-life
is an enigma ever for many.

Varchaswi L. Putcha

SHAWL

That thing slithers and unfolds into hoods
and crawls around your neck, alas, like a noose!
As if breathing ignorance and hissing arrogance
it sneaks its way on your torso in haughtiness!

The over zeal in your heart and the vanity in your stiff-neck
expand your thorax trying to fit into that cloak
The swelters you felt under the adorned moult
give shelter to the amour-propre that's built

The claps for you on the decorated daises
and the pats on you at simmering banquets
shoo you into snake-pit of shawl
that kill your skills of life in a long haul

That clever cover turns you sultriest
and veils your nescience in its best
It cares you if you care its pious caresses
If you bury in its coziness, there lies your Carcass

Varchaswi L. Putcha

STAY SAFE

By now, what is well known to all is Covid
What pounces unbeknownst is also Covid

Pandemics in yore were person-centric
this novel one doth corrode very social fabric

All ideologies crumbled down to incertitude
and all the philosophies fumbled with ineptitude

and got crunched under its tentacles, new
highlighting Darwin's survival of the fittest few

Shrines once conched and echoed panegyric
Now barren, succumbing to a tragic covidal magic

Regionalism and religions proved to be a big myth
so also haves and have-nots, when new strains take a birth

No cure yet, albeit an arrival of vaccine authentic
till then masking and safe-distancing should be our lives' rubric

HILARIOUS GALES

A wafting zephyr suddenly hit hard my heart this dusk Made me peek into the window to find nature's brusque

It's the bouncy virgin rain hitting my flower pots at balcony
Hoisting a licorice pain soothing my heart of melancholy

Gales of fragrance tickled my spirits up and up
As the first splash drizzled straight in to my open lap

A thunder, peculiar to the season, struck a bit yonder
A baffled cuckoo fluttered away winding up a song of it's lore

To beat the pervading chill that transfused my sill
My honey appeared with a cup of hot tea, to my thrill

Climates at times keep the soul mates free from feuds
Granting blooms of hugs sending scents of blissful moods

Subdued light slowly lead me by hand to join the boudoir
On the top, these gusty winds gouged a bard in me, hurrah

Varchaswi L. Putcha

BRUSH

I splashed high
some sapphire hues... they made the sky!

Below, I daubed some light greens...
they became emerald meadows!

A wee behind,
I sprayed thick greens to form dense forests!

I further whitewashed for radiance On the silvery dancing Levin,
That usurped the bouncing blue brooks and rills,

Oh! there I spilled out few black blotches,
That shaped into little birds to fly in the azures

Yeah...I got now in my lap a beautiful oeuvre
of stunning hues!

While setting ready my elegant easel for the art gallery......
ah, two drops of tears dribbled down my eyes...

like two parallel streams of cool 'joy' and burning 'pain'!

Varchaswi L. Putcha

'Joy', for having my brush pullulated into lush green foliage
'Pain', for the lamentation of wild plantations under shrinkage

Varchaswi L. Putcha

POOR SPARROW

I ask that restive parrot jingling and jarring
to sojourn there a while on its bough, swaying

I demand that royal swan sashaying in the welkin milks
to stick to its gargantuan status pious always

I heckle at the peacock to wander a bit yonder
who saunters in pompous plumage, being a vaunter

I demand the cuckoos to adjourn their slurring coos
trying to prune the tune of the new autumn to let loose

but, I welcome the little sparrow, an extinguishing bird
facing injury in the hands of gadgetry halberd

Varchaswi L. Putcha

IN THE FIST OF TIMES...!

You have traces of capturing time
first in the fists of fetus
It's an inexplicable enigma
Known since your empty mouthed smiles
as to whether you hold bridle of it
or let glide through fistfuls

As you unfold thy fists
pride sets on you that
you can maneuver the wheel of time
or apply breaks to it, only in illusion!
Till what length you think you umbilical cord
scaled the game of time so as to boast
that you tucked in your waist
the bunch of keys of 'time machine'?

Lo! Time may plod or ride
crawl or swirl in pure volition!
Conquering time or giving up time
are words roll from us free
in its grand game of glee
Not having smacked fully of 'between the life'
you look at 'beyond the life'

Varchaswi L. Putcha

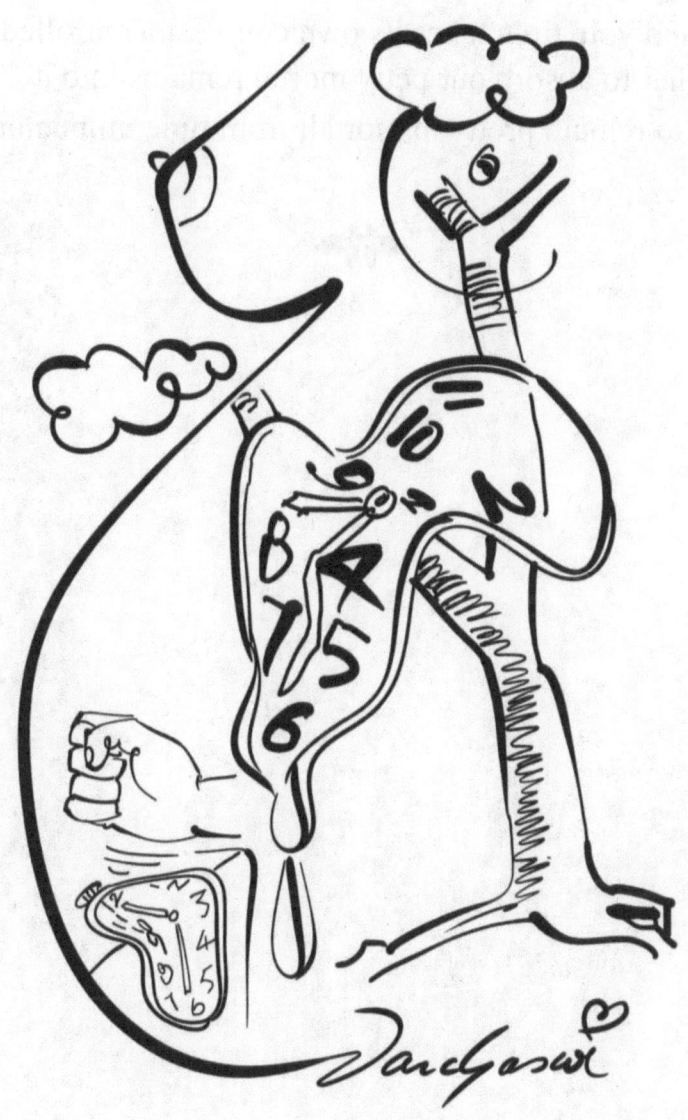

By the time you feel a capture of time into your fists
they lay bare and pale sans life!
Mind you, time takes its own course uncontrolled
either to absorb our petty mortal remains into it
or to remain pretty immortal, from time immemorial!

Varchaswi L. Putcha

MIGRANT BIRD AT NELAPATTU

We, the poor birds know
that you keep us always in low;
But, have you ever tried twittering with parrots?
Ever shared your words with sparrows?
Ever befriended squawking peacock?
Ever your mind pregnant with the migrant birds?

Hey! Focus on us, a while, who are seen seldom in your scene
Am sure, your spirits elate like a flight, of migrant birds!
And emit shimmering radiance like our wide stretched white wings
Teach darting skills like our long darting beaks
Sing a sonorous song of solidarity like our winged community;

Being fledged afresh, your heart effaces empyrean distances, in efficacy
Manifests as a coolest zone for a best sojourn;
And the decency of colony of birds descends on you;
And like our bowers, made of stems and stalks, That
Shoot or sprout amorous hearts- shower mirth!

Varchaswi L. Putcha

Wings Of A Free Bard

You will catch hold of a fleshy-fish of passion and
love all your indolence under the claws of chills
melts in the lukewarm flames of 'poesies on
Flamingos ' Dear Sirs-
Harken us for a nice microcosm
Clean the highways of Welkins for pelicans Roll out
verdant carpets for common cranes
See that rivulets run and squirm like a humming birds
Get creaks and brooks into manifolds, to harbor us

Do all this to us
and we swear in return
that we relinquish our foreign citizenship and pretty
settle at Nelapattu!

(Nelapattu is a place of birds' sanctuary near 'Pulikat lake'
in Nellore District, A.P., India)

TRAIN THE THOUGHTS

The clumsy train of thoughts halts only to resume foraying
At times   it dwells on an amazing maze of musings
Cruises into   the lap of flora and fauna, once
Stops, thinks and back to things worldly, in a bounce
Lo, a travelling mind thus keeps us fit in a mental recycling

                                     (in 'limerick' format)

Varchaswi L. Putcha

GAIETY OF MY CITY

'Hello...';
'Isn't that how normally you address, my dear?
'Hi Hyderabad...!' too is a word of resonance, trust me here

The very name of Hyderabad hoists happiest havens
and the very climate culls thrills of chilling passions

Take a look at the whole city, from a slum to a plum place
And go raptures in capturing the city's captivating grace

It homes penniless and powerful on an equal plank
and the folks are great, gorgeous, genial and too frank

Penning poesy on my Hyderabad is like drooling for biryani,
and a tete-a-tete with dudes is like slurping a hot chai, Irani

Varchaswi L. Putcha

Rich cultures and skilled treasure troves were built in galore
from Satavahanas to Kakathiyas to Sultanates and more;

From Shahis or Jahis to Nijams to today's elected Nethas
That makes the place a 'paradise' to live in, with fiestas

Flourished once upon a time as Bhagyanagar and now blossomed into Hyderabad
Turned into 'twins' with Secunderabad and now a 'trinity' with Cyberabad

My city is a lovely diversity with a remarkable unity coupled with humanity
Lastly, it's a gaiety-metro of artists and poets with ambrosial talents aplenty

Varchaswi L. Putcha

WAVELENGTHS AT SECONCERTS

They gush-out
and they rush-in, the best
as I look at the seas!
That wave after wave so pleases
enticing me with its troughs and crests
and presents me lovely sonnets
Am sure those wave- lengths
can't be deciphered in a lesson of physics
nor be evaluated under a sort of mathematics
yet that concurs with our wave-lengths!

They chill out
and blow in, sweet
while I saunter in the facade!
I seize with ease those breezes, awed
I love losing in the maze of those waves
bringing full of fragrances waft-in from boughs
Wave after wave, a bit vibrant
pampers my inner bon vivant
carrying me to a world of Shangri-La
thus mingling our wave-lengths hoo-la-la!

Varchaswi L. Putcha

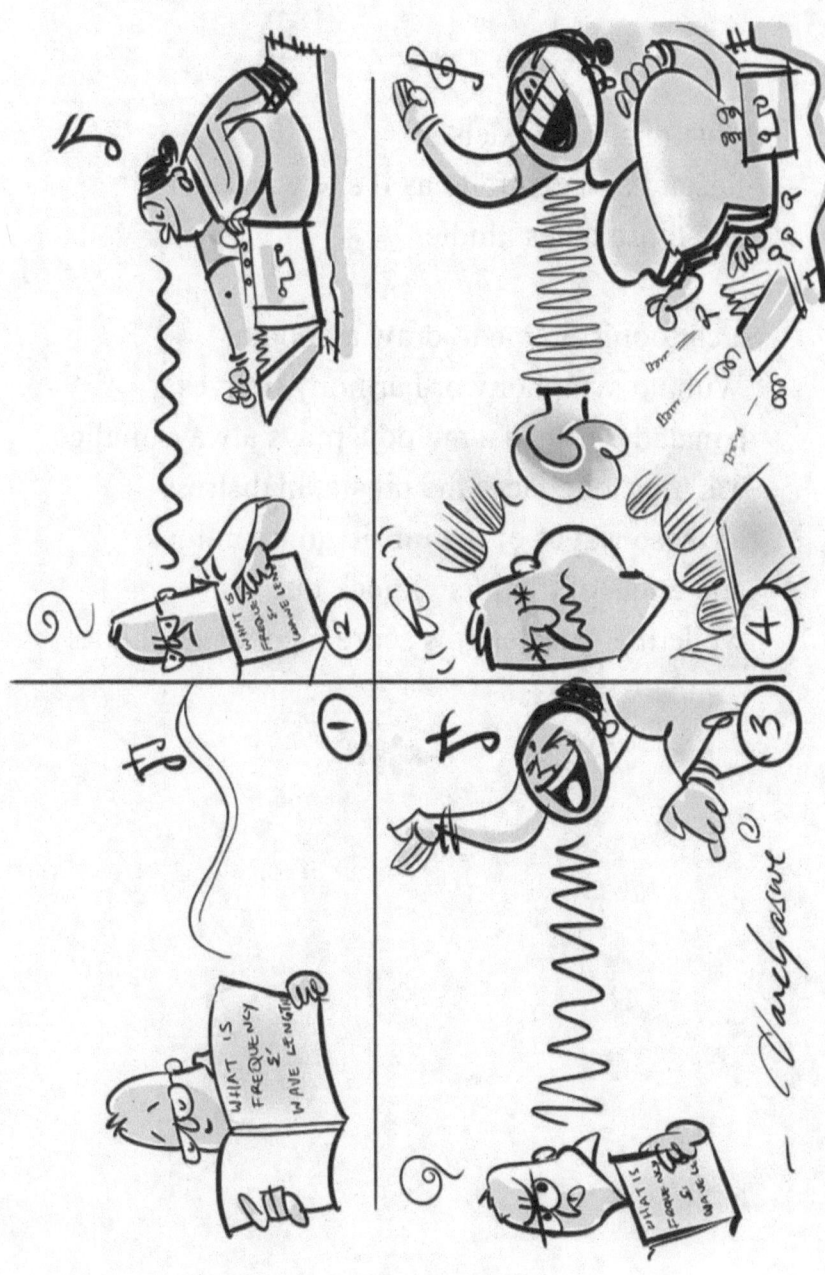

That mistress yodels
falsetto and contralto as if she wails
and those tunes kindle

a cartoonist in me to draw a doodle!
With no symphony or harmony in lives,
a malady instead a melody, plays always malice
Yet he alone faces the music, in distress
as these waves of the music go tremulous
and bouts of tremors   knock out him
while the wavelengths score incoherent chime!

YOGA AND ISOLATION

When the life goes berserk and plays foul
embrace mother nature that sanitizes a poor soul

Sit up in the thick meadows beneath
and canopies of green bushes zenith

And where fresh breaths of pranayama phase
assimilate with the therapeutic herbal breeze

Take permit from it that distances us physically
where an isolation is prescribed invariably

Arrange yourself a rendezvous
with the nature to remove the woe

where an aura of corona is banished
and where all sneezes of strains are smashed
See that the pains of pandemics cease
and shatters into wilderness or universe!

Once in a while, isolate yourself under yogic den
Physically or psychologically avoid go murky and mundane

Varchaswi L. Putcha

TOLLS IN 'NOOSE' PAPER

Your waking up into dawn can't be by your proxy
you ought to do it on your own, you see

None can breathe your breath, my dear pal
for, that's you alone ought to breathe for survival

None can fight your battle in the field
as you only have wielded the sword and shield

Remember you are pretty global yet a tiny fry
when all hugs go dry and hangouts are a far cry

Agreed you are a wandering albatross yet a wingless
Though seemingly a juggernaut, you remain naught at times

Today's prideful number on one's card, aadhaar
may get flashed, if played unsafe, on his sepulcher

One may be billionaire, a great
but won't measure oneself beyond six, in feet

Varchaswi L. Putcha

Last breathes are unpredictable, in terms usual
but last rites also lost sights in seasons, covidal

The terrific altar may be a lofty mountain moor
or a fateful sitting-rock the next door

Stop counting tolls and quarantines in news papers
on the cross-roads of the unchecked viruses

Though rest of life forebodes 'bitter' half
Better accustom to dictates of better-half

Tear away the 'noose' paper giving fears and tears
Smile away the tensions with precautions, my dears

Varchaswi L. Putcha

ONLINE CLASSES

Success-game of life needs you to learn it from A to Z
As a kid you plod over A, B, C, D   during infancy
amid dreams of parents sowed in your little head;
They struggle and wriggle to set your life so cozy

Unmindful of your goal, you will be driven crazy
from nest to new vistas, in many a twist of life's mystery
realizing slowly that studies sans riches go awry
Promises luring KG to PG free, prove a utopian theory
With no light at the end of the pandemic tunnel, so scary
you need added riches to attend classes going virtual

As usual, you ought to cough up all your fees squarely
strains may be tentative yet sales of academics are
perpetual

We brag that our globe became so tiny a village
Whether online or offline, clean education here is a mirage

Varchaswi L. Putcha

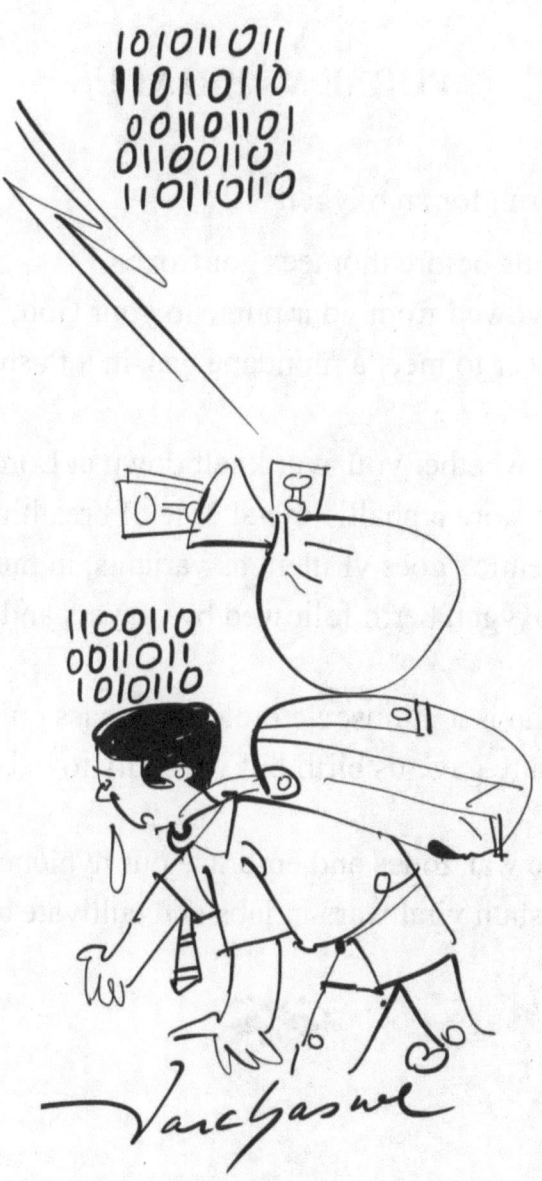

PURSE Vs PRIAPUS

Run, run, run for an oxygen
Save our souls before thoraces got frozen
What you avowed from your purse to your God, in cash
Now disappear to meet a mundane gas, in a flash

Don't know whether you ever knelt down at Lord Priapus
But, keep in store a phallic metal case of breathing gas
When pandemic goes virulent as variants, in menace
Grab your oxygen berth followed by prayers and penance

After all, man is a minuscule biological mass on the earth
Mother-Nature gave us birth but we badly toyed with it in mirth
Scrap all the war zones and embrace our hygiene zone
It's time to shun viral wars in labs and cultivate a peace-hormone

Varchaswi L. Putcha

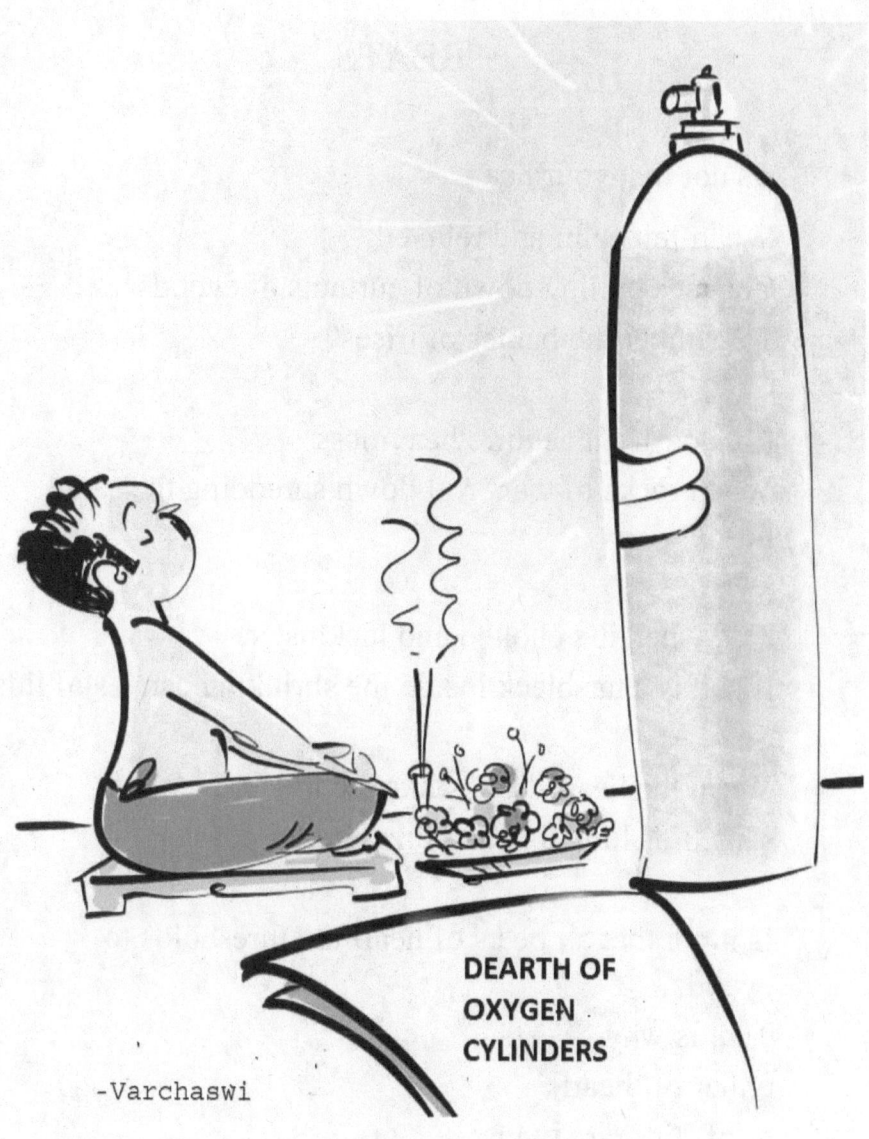

BEATS

Is not that your heart
When felt calm and relaxed
Chooses pulling down of curtains of eyelids
To pamper the babies of irises?

Lo, doesn't it acquire heaviness
When rocks of tears roll down shredding the same lids

And when it's choked and lackluster,
It paints a tar-black inside the shrinking canvas of lids

When the heart droops like a child
same lids look lost in a dizzy roller coaster;

Is it not that all beats of heart are thresholds to eyelids?
That is why - beats
either of 'hearts'
or of 'lids' are twins
that give you notes of time passing-by
reflecting your sublime catharses.

Varchaswi L. Putcha

BOOKLET

When I take a new poetry book into hands
It's wrapper slowly fades away into a stage-screen
while I unclad the lines in the book into a story-board;
So also all the pages, one by one, into a maze of characters

Only then the river-let of booklet flows into mind
Easing out sailing the currents of text and context
I sail, smack, smooch and scintillate with the
articulates of the write

As the essence of the book, in hand
Gives effervescence of inexplicable thrill and knowledge
and as the tome widens the dome of wisdom, in grand
Those gushes of epitome quench me as a salvage!

Varchaswi L. Putcha

I AM

Pity that I am not identified as a part of ever expanding universe
Pity that I am not identified as descendent of a twinkling star
Pity that I am not identified particle in crawling cosmos
Pity that I am not identified as neither a telling time nor an open space
Pity that I am not identified as casual chromosome too
Nor was I identified as flesh and blood at least
Not even as a being with intangible colorless grey matter
Not identified as a fire to scorch
Not even as a wind to feel
Not at least as a fist of dust
Not as a human before a human
Not as a joy of you
Not as a nest of you
Not as a promise of you
Not as neighborhood
Not as close dude ...!

Varchaswi L. Putcha

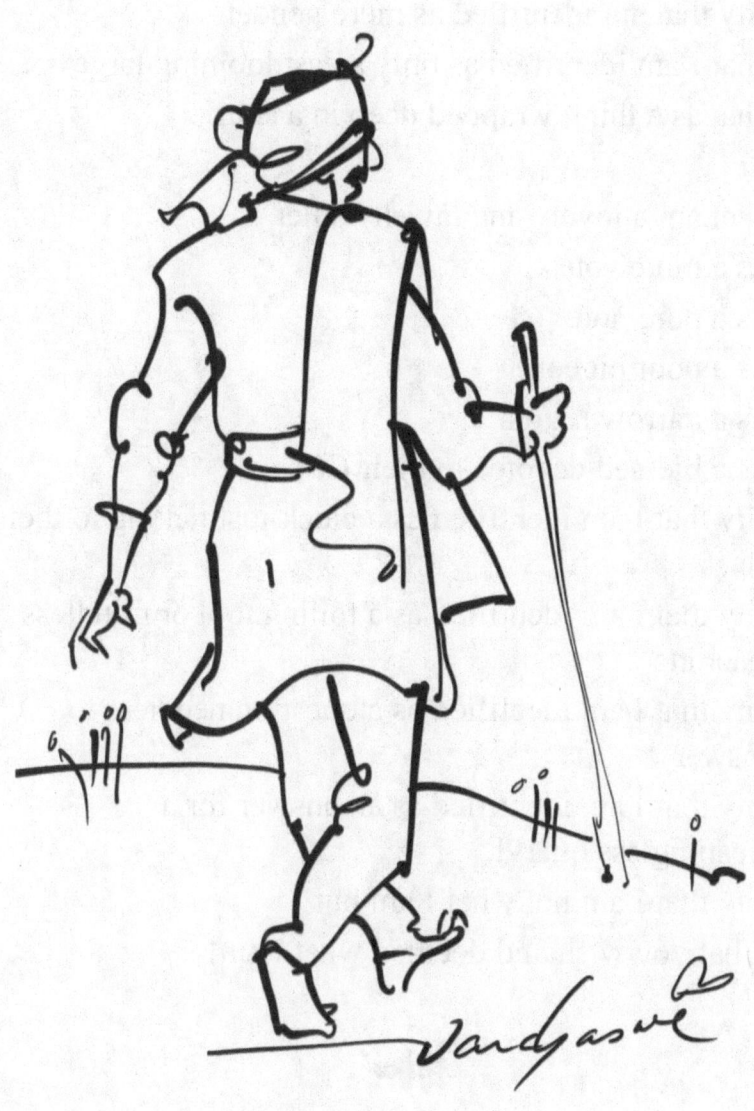

Pity that am identified as some color painted by blindness
Pity that am identified as mere gender
That I am identified as only a cast looming large
That as a thing wrapped deep in a skin

That am a lovely and lavish wallet
As a mute vote
As a pure note
As a poor pigeon
As a narrow region
As a blessed devotee to their Gods
Pity that I am identified as a clock just ticking to their tunes
Pity that I am identified as a toiling tool or mindless machine
Pity that I am identified as a question needless to answer
Pity that I am identified as an answer for a meaningless query!
Pity that I am not what I am but
What you wish and decided what I am!

Varchaswi L. Putcha

BEST ACTION

A cine star who had liposuction
To act in a film of princely portion
A poet mended a bit his way
Got a good readership hooray
Lo, both made their best version

       (A limerick)

Varchaswi L. Putcha

'ONE MORE ROUND' OF A LIMERICK

My dude in the next chair
pampered me pouring slyness into my beer
He munched my secrets
I too drank his regrets
Under dim lights, love or war is fair.

Varchaswi L. Putcha

A DROP

I am a bubble,
At your tip of your nail.
I am a tiny pearl,
To accept your offered kiss.
I am a river carrier
When you allow me to flow.
I am a sturdy cascade
In capturing your glow.
I am the massive seas,
If you sail with my every wave.
I am the dripping nectar,
If you savor my sweet taste.
I will be the humongous hurricane
If you dare snuff me out, as if I am a drop.

Varchaswi L. Putcha

APPLICATION

Hurl at me your eyeball once from there
I will roll out a season of spring at your façade

Spark a hint of a smile at your threshold
I will shine like a rainbow at your bough

Shower your gait and gaiety on me
I will deluge you with splashy tides of my heart beats

Infuse my heart with your ambrosial loyalty
I will be a love-song that unleashes your loneliness

Grant me an accepting big hug
I incarnate as your serpent god you adore

Varchaswi L. Putcha

'CELL' PHONE

What a 'smart friend' you are
Not even pushing out a 'smiley'
To my screen nowadays!
How Can I keep myself 'charged'?

'No space'
in your 'drive'?
what can I do
except to put my thumbs down?

You are gluttonous
And crave for more RAM.
Yes, you ate out full
of my 'memory chip'.

You love
the cover, outer!
And you ignore the
sumptuous 'Intel inside'.

Varchaswi L. Putcha

You have all eyes
both front and back, to click
whether selfie or themie or groupie
stop spam with your cam.

Yes, you are
my 'android'
The deity and key
Showing the way, day to day;
unmindful of life- turn
Bravo, Cell is a 'life' and life is a 'cell'

OF DOVES

On some roof-top or a storey
and on walls and on parapets
Murmuring and munching
speaking, swirling and sashaying
squeaking and shrieking
Chirping, fluttering and flaunting

No strife and no grief
Now here and ere there
No bustles and no bullets
No resident permanent
And none for rent
No registrations and no reservations
No fissures or seizures

May be, their attitudes
Are in high altitudes.

(A translation from Telugu penned by Shri Uppaluri Atreya Sarma, Editor museindia.com)

Varchaswi L. Putcha

SLITHERED MIRROR

Let the crowds pelt stones in huge numbers and let the enemies slice
the bodies with daggers that may not inflict injuries

But those very close to our hearts prattle an offending brittle-word that is enough to break tender hearts like a mirror that slithered

A wreaked piece of necklace though tied up in a knot may not retain its grace
and ceases into a naught

(Translation of a Telugu poem written by Poet Asha Raju)

Varchaswi L. Putcha

EACH ARTICLE A PENNY!

I know him as a kid

Close to my heart since childhood with his unique and articulated voice and with the affectionate moonlit eyes

He goes hawking by cycling in the old city lanes carrying the chattel on his neck and shoulder planes

Hark the announcement 'Each article a penny'

Used to park we kids around him in numbers many

Combs, mirrors, pins, scissors, nail cutters...

Snows, powders, soaps ... and what not bro! Grab anything for a paltry penny

All is local made in my lovely Hyderabad

Really a mobile retailer satiating the poor man's need

It's like an aftermath of the lashed-out rains

When he left after a swept-out sales in all those lanes

He just looks like a materialist at his best

without sporting a Bindi on forehead or a hat or pagidi on his pate to test

For me he's a glamour hero nearer or a great street warrior ever

***

Varchaswi L. Putcha

Wings Of A Free Bard

In my adolescence, his slogan rang differently 'Each article two rupees only…'
With a metamorphosis into an old motor bike
Carrying nothing short of an exhibition coolly…
Albeit we didn't form huge crowds over there
Those calls of walking super-bazaar transmit waves of clarinets clear

***

After a long span….

The other day that vendor descended in an old Suzuki trolley announcing 'Each article twenty rupees only' stuffed with all the sundry
Come any number of super bazaars, Spensers, multiplexes or wall-marts
His ringing echoes of 'each article….'
Goes un-infringed by any sorts
Like Kamadhenu, a mythological cow or like a Kalpavriksha, a desire tree
To a common man, in my pious Nation till it crosses the line of poverty

(A translation of Telugu poem penned by Dr SVSatyanarayana, the erstwhile Vice Chancellor of Telugu Varsity, Hyderabad)

A FOOT-PATH APPEARS

Just have a siesta
You will get a way-out Yes, a way-out even in the thickest of the thicket
Despite at the darkest-abode of jungle
You will find a faintest ray of way!

Where the life itself is a jungle
and where the life itself is a dilapidated city;
What a human being has to do-
Take out and hold the flambeau of heart and start moving!
Trust, nothing is route-less!
For sure, you get a paddle to cross the river Keep on your searching
Search after search is the 'life'
We walk in the mountainous mountains full of hillocks that are endless;
Simply feel them cool as greens of rocks and sure you find from blues a moon beam
Pretty squat somewhere and open a saccule of sorrows and bite a morsel there from-
Is everything is like this, always? The sun and moon are atop

Varchaswi L. Putcha

Wings Of A Free Bard

Thereat, the empyreans and Welkins too
Lo, the human being stands at the beneath
A human being standing solid and exquisite
Yes, a human being, who can find a solution;
And yes, a human-life, built by a human being,
A 'human' who is a replicate of nature-

Human beings and nature both are same
Certainly a route shoots up
like a sprout of Palmyra
and one brook-like foot path emerges
Then, shoulder your life-palanquin and take up a procession to reach
all the corners around uttering "ohom…ohom"!

(Translation of Telugu poem penned by Dr.K.Siva Reddy, a renowned poet)

Varchaswi L. Putcha

A LITTLE WHILE

All the ferries pretty well
go asleep in the lap of a river
musing those bustling twilights of yesterday

There around an old fisherman pitches
a bait into the water body after
dismantling the misty blanket wrapped up
by the river

Still the hamlet
skirting the river-bank, yonder
lies snuggled under a blanket of fog slipping
more into its sleep
And there, the Sun creeps up holding firmly
the firmament and the rivulet like a
gleefully playing little fellow

All the sparrows chirrup heartily parting themselves
from the solitudes of the lushly and bushy foliage

Hey, please don't come this side for a little while, till
those sparrows, the stream, the Sun
and the welkin play to the hilt
and till their bodies fully soaked.

(Translation of Telugu poem penned by Afsar Mohammed, a renowned poet)

Varchaswi L. Putcha

THE RAIN-BOW THAT LOVED ME

A rainy season
Unforeseen…
dismounted inside me
fluttering its wings!

Without my knowledge
it engulfed all my limbs,
unnerved my vision and hearken!

Unfolding the rainbow-hood,
it danced in my bed
smearing me with an eighth color!

Ah, In that twilight …
pennons of orgasmic splash
in white brilliance….
in the form of 'arch of light'
witch-crafted me!

My lips closed under those
unfamiliar ambrosial hers
fetched from the cirrus
made me
a tad stupefied!

Varchaswi L. Putcha

Wings Of A Free Bard

In the effulgence of her body
the rain-bow I braced
from the posy,
down to the bud pivot
still surprisingly gleams within me.

(Translation from Telugu penned by Late Sri Devipriya, a renowned poet and author.)

AMARANTH

Oh! Maybe, an Amaranth that bloomed in the blues;
Or a love poem that struck like a lightning in a poet,
Yet, both turned a single 'you' and filled my heart!
Oh! May be……
Your figure of a divine-lamp
And your laughter of newborn-stars
Filled my eyes with full of moonlight
Oh! May be……
Hey! Come here -
while your milky cheeks sprout and spring blushes
And do come -
while your azure wispy hairs play with zephyrs
Do come like a Royal swan with clinking anklets
Oh! May be……
You are the lightning that rippled dreams
in the placid clouds of mine
It's only you who serenade romantic songs on my lute of life
While exuding nectar in every single word,
Oh, Come my dear prince of classics!
Oh! May be……

(Translation of Telugu song penned by late Dr. Dasarathi, eminent cine lyricist)

Varchaswi L. Putcha

KASTURI VIJAYAM

📞 00-91 95150 54998
KASTURIVIJAYAM@GMAIL.COM

SUPPORTS

- PUBLISH YOUR BOOK AS YOUR OWN PUBLISHER.

- PAPERBACK & E-BOOK SELF-PUBLISHING

- SUPPORT PRINT ON-DEMAND.

- YOUR PRINTED BOOKS AVAILABLE AROUND THE WORLD.

- EASY TO MANAGE YOUR BOOK'S LOGISTICS AND TRACK YOUR REPORTING.

www.ingramcontent.com/pod-product-compliance
Lightning Source LLC
LaVergne TN
LVHW030322070526
838199LV00069B/6537